I0605180

Strange Creatures in the Bible

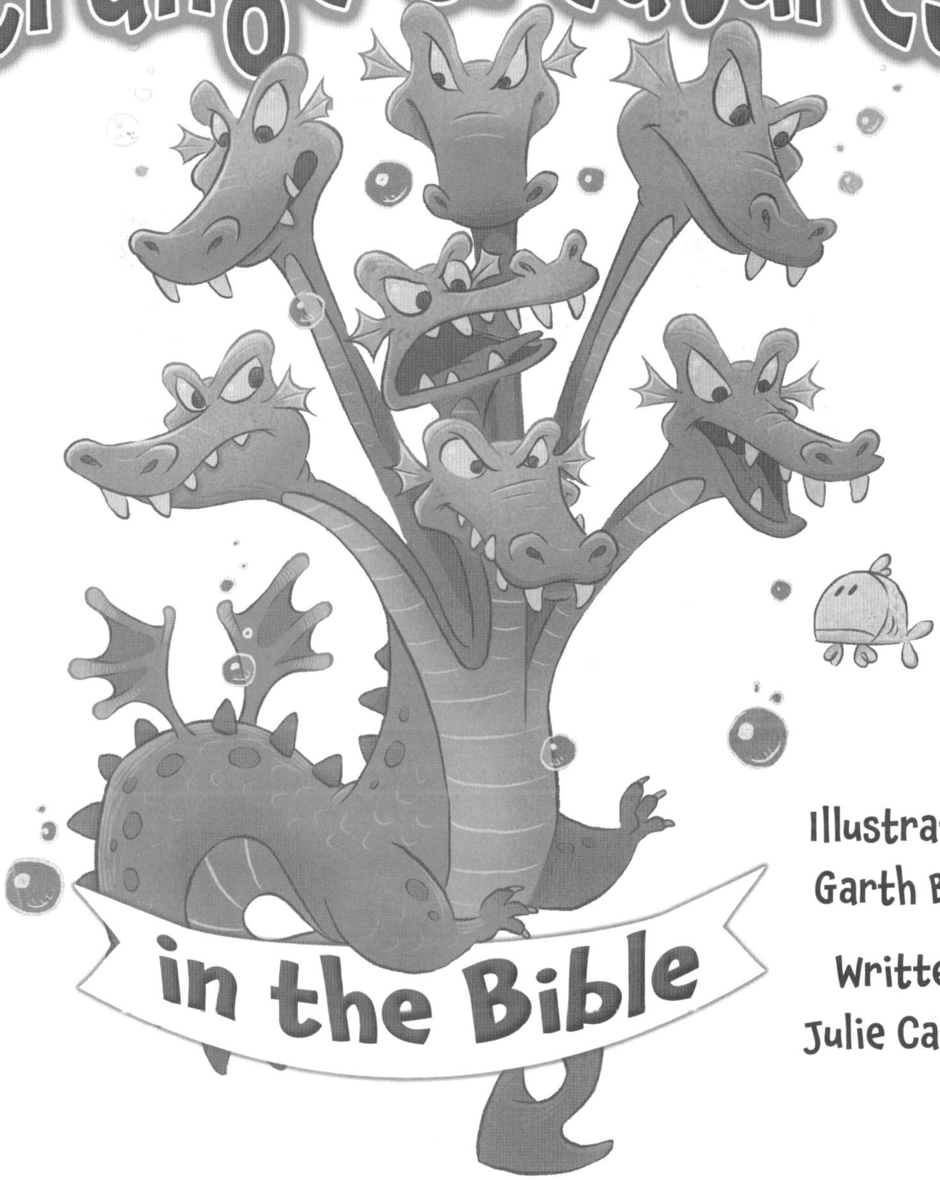

Illustrated by
Garth Bruner

Written by
Julie Campbell

Scripture quotations marked (KJV) are taken from the Holy Bible, King James Version. Public domain.

Scripture quotations marked (NIV) are taken from The Holy Bible, New International Version® NIV®
Copyright © 1973, 1978, 1984, 2011 by Biblica, Inc. Used with permission. All rights reserved worldwide.

The purchase of this coloring book grants you the rights to photocopy the contents for classroom use.
Notice: It is unlawful to copy these pages for resale purposes. Copy permission is for private use only.

Copyright © 2025 Warner Press, Inc. All rights reserved. Made in USA

30580PO100000051

Did you know there are strange creatures mentioned in the Bible?
Take **leviathan**, for instance. While we don't know for sure,
this amazing beast was possibly a fierce sea monster-like creature!

© 2025 Warner Press, Inc All rights reserved E5093

Three books of the Bible mention leviathan: Job (chapters 3 and 41), Psalm (74:14; 104:26), and Isaiah (27:1).

Use the number code to discover some of the characteristics of this frightening creature.

1. According to Isaiah 27:1 (KJV), leviathan is compared to a ___ ___ ___ ___ ___ ___.
   1 6 4 3 2 5

2. Job 41:9 (NIV) says the mere sight of leviathan is
   ___ ___ ___ ___ ___ ___ ___ ___ ___ ___ ___ ___ .
   2 7 9 6 8 2 11 9 6 10 5 3

3. ___ ___ ___ ___ ___ pours from leviathan's ___ ___ ___ ___ ___ ___ ___ ___ .
   12 14 2 13 9 — 5 2 12 15 6 10 16 12
   (from Job 41:20 NIV)

4. Leviathan is a creature without ___ ___ ___ ___ . (from Job 41:33 NIV).
   17 9 4 6

5. ___ ___ ___ ___ ___ ___ and ___ ___ ___ ___ ___ ___ have no effect
   12 11 2 6 1 12 — 12 8 9 4 6 12
   on leviathan. (from Job 41:26 NIV)

© 2025 Warner Press, Inc All rights reserved E5093

Another huge beast mentioned in the Book of Job is the **behemoth** (Job 40:15–24). Some Bible scholars believe this creature could have looked like a woolly mammoth, while others think it might have been a hippopotamus or a dinosaur.

© 2025 Warner Press, Inc All rights reserved E5093

Complete the crossword puzzle to learn more about the behemoth.

ACROSS:

2. It is ______ to capture. (Job 40:24 NIV)

5. Its limbs are like rods of _______. (Job 40:18 NIV)

6. Its tail sways like a _______. (Job 40:17 NIV)

8. A raging _________ does not alarm it. (Job 40:23 NIV)

9. It lies under the _____ plants. (Job 40:21 NIV)

DOWN:

1. Its bones are like tubes of ________. (Job 40:18 NIV)

3. It ranks _______ among the works of God. (Job 40:19 NIV)

4. The muscles of its belly are ________. (Job 40:16 NIV)

7. It feeds on ________ like an ox. (Job 40:15 NIV)

© 2025 Warner Press, Inc All rights reserved E5093

Did you know **dragons** are mentioned over 30 times
in the King James version of the Bible?
These creatures are often described as fierce and fire-breathing!

© 2025 Warner Press, Inc All rights reserved E5093

Leviathan, the creature we learned about on pages 2 and 3, had some dragon-like qualities.

Use the symbol code to discover how the Bible describes it.

1. Its snorting throws out ___ ___ ___ ___ ___ ___ ___

of ___ ___ ___ ___ ___ . (Job 41:18 NIV)

2. ___ ___ ___ ___ ___ ___ stream from its ___ ___ ___ ___ ___;

___ ___ ___ ___ ___ ___ of ___ ___ ___ ___ shoot out. (Job 41:19 NIV)

3. Its ___ ___ ___ ___ ___ ___ sets coals ablaze. (Job 41:21 NIV)

© 2025 Warner Press, Inc All rights reserved E5093

While you may not think **unicorns** are real, they are mentioned in the Bible! They probably looked more like this brawny, powerful, one-horned creature. (See Numbers 24:8 KJV; Isaiah 34:7 KJV.)

© 2025 Warner Press, Inc All rights reserved E5093

Find your way through the maze to the unicorn.

© 2025 Warner Press, Inc All rights reserved E5093

In Deuteronomy 14:5 KJV, the **pygarg** is among a list of biblical animals.
Some Bible experts believe this creature
was a type of ancient antelope with twisted horns.

© 2025 Warner Press, Inc All rights reserved E5093

What are the names of the other animals mentioned in Deuteronomy 14:5 (KJV)?

Decode the animals' names using the phone buttons. The number below each line in the puzzle tells you which button to use. Then pick a letter and write it on the line to form a word. Hint: You may have to try more than once to find the right letters! Look up the scripture if you need help!

1	2 ABC	3 DEF
4 GHI	5 JKL	6 MNO
7 PQRS	8 TUV	9 WXYZ
*	0	#

__ __ __ __
4 2 7 8

__ __ __ __ __ __ __
7 6 3 2 8 2 5

__ __ __ __ __ __ __ __ __ __
3 2 5 5 6 9 3 3 3 7

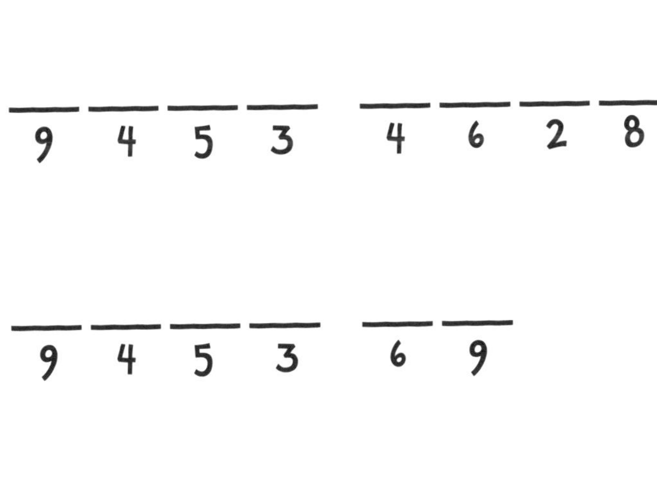

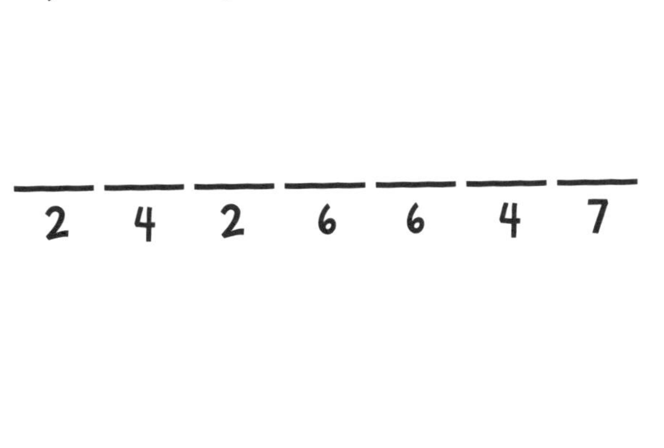

© 2025 Warner Press, Inc All rights reserved E5093

Have you heard the story of the **talking donkey** in Numbers 22:21–35?
The donkey's owner was a wicked prophet named Balaam.

© 2025 Warner Press, Inc All rights reserved E5093

When Balaam disobeyed God's instructions, God sent an angel to stand in the donkey's way. Balaam couldn't see the angel, so he kept beating the poor donkey every time it stopped!

What question did the donkey ask Balaam?

Cross out the names of fruits and animals.
Write the remaining words in order on the lines to read the Bible verse.

strawberry	What	crocodile	have
watermelon	skunk	I	apple
done	panda	lime	cherry
lemon	fox	to	tiger
eagle	you	banana	elephant
to	walrus	otter	sheep
zebra	pear	make	orange
you	horse	blueberry	grape
lion	beat	hippo	snake
pineapple	dog		me

________ ________ ____

________ ______ ________ _____

________ ______ ________ _____?

Numbers 22:28 (NIV)

© 2025 Warner Press, Inc All rights reserved E5093

In the Garden of Eden, the devil revealed himself as a **talking serpent** and convinced Eve to disobey God!

© 2025 Warner Press, Inc All rights reserved E5093

This is what the serpent said to Eve: Did God really say, "You must not eat from any tree in the garden?" (Genesis 3:1 NIV)

Circle the underlined words hidden in the puzzle.

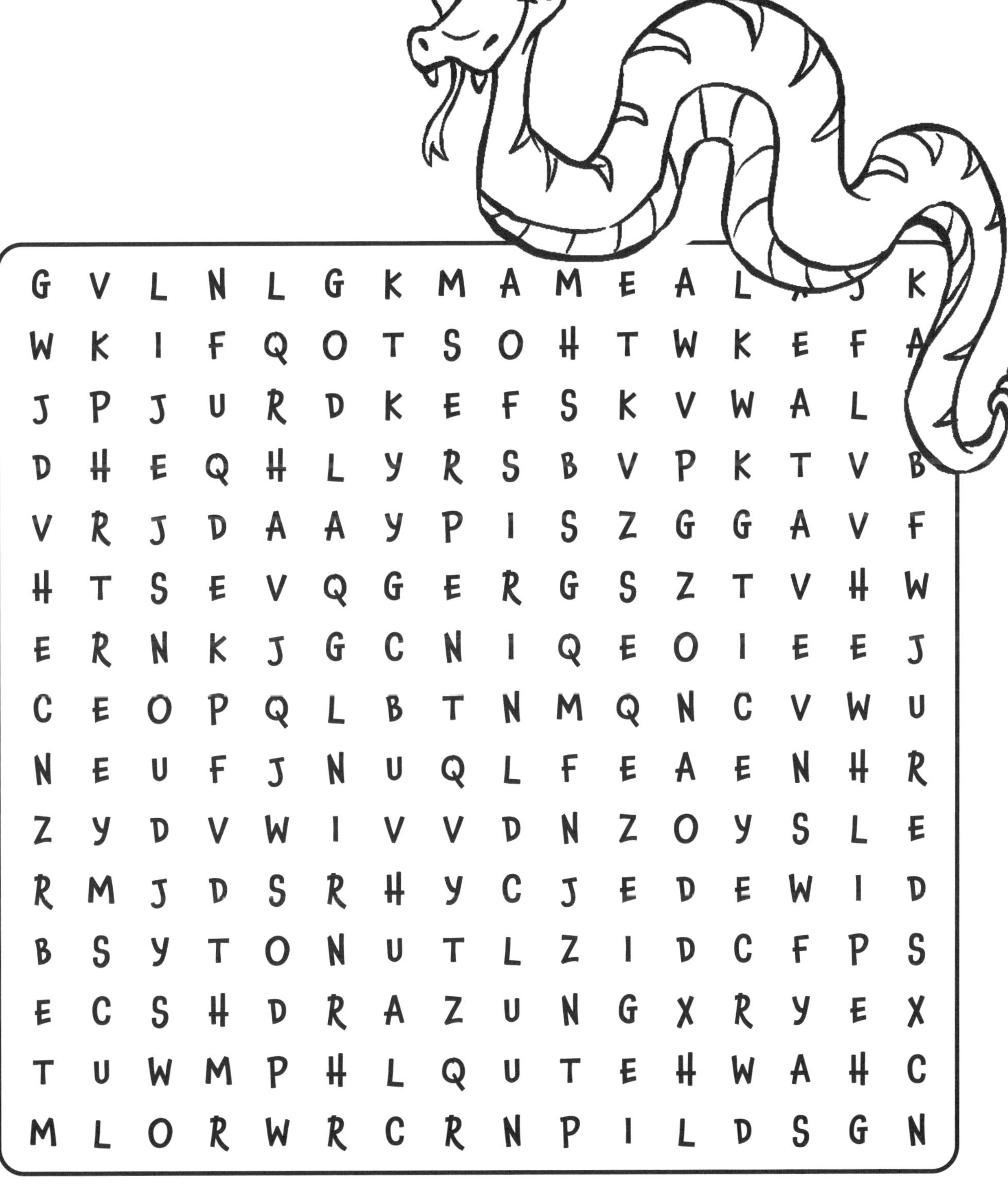

© 2025 Warner Press, Inc All rights reserved E5093

Answers

Page 3

1. **dragon**
2. **overpowering**
3. **smoke** and **nostrils**
4. **fear**
5. **swords** and **spears**

Page 5

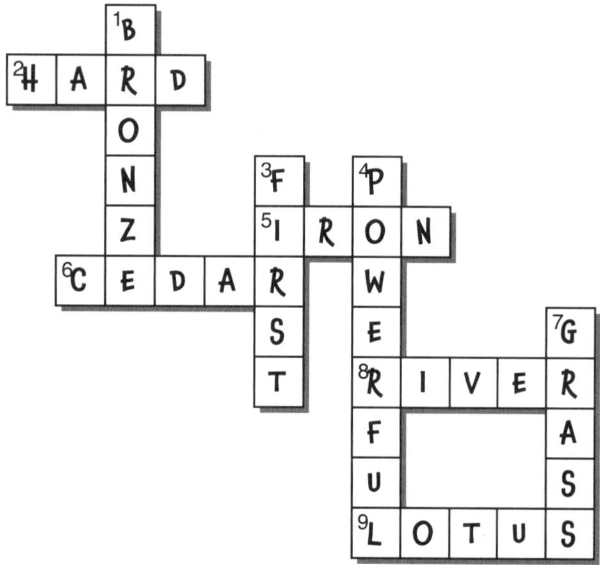

Page 7

1. **flashes, light**
2. **Flames, mouth; sparks, fire**
3. **breath**

Page 9

Page 11

1. **hart** 2. **roebuck** 3. **fallow deer**
4. **wild goat** 5. **wild ox** 6. **chamois**

Page 13

What have I done to you to make you beat me?

Page 15

G	V	L	N	L	G	K	M	A	M	E	A	L	X	J	K
W	K	I	F	Q	O	T	S	O	H	T	W	K	E	F	A
J	P	J	U	R	D	K	E	F	S	K	V	W	A	L	W
D	H	E	Q	H	L	Y	R	S	B	V	P	K	T	V	B
V	R	J	D	A	A	Y	P	I	S	Z	G	G	A	V	F
H	T	S	E	V	Q	G	E	R	G	S	Z	T	V	H	W
E	R	N	K	J	G	C	N	I	Q	E	O	I	E	E	J
C	E	O	P	Q	L	B	T	N	M	Q	N	C	V	W	U
N	E	U	F	J	N	U	Q	L	F	E	A	E	N	H	R
Z	Y	D	V	W	I	V	V	D	N	Z	O	Y	S	L	E
R	M	J	D	S	R	H	Y	C	J	E	D	E	W	I	D
B	S	Y	T	O	N	U	T	L	Z	I	D	C	F	P	S
E	C	S	H	D	R	A	Z	U	N	G	X	R	Y	E	X
T	U	W	M	P	H	L	Q	U	T	E	H	W	A	H	C
M	L	O	R	W	R	C	R	N	P	I	L	D	S	G	N

© 2025 Warner Press, Inc All rights reserved E5093